P9-DTL-326

★ SPORTS STARS ★

DON SHULA

FOOTBALL'S WINNINGEST COACH

By R. Conrad Stein

 CHILDRENS PRESS ®
CHICAGO

Allen County Public Library
900 Webster Street
PO Box 2270
Fort Wayne, IN 46801-2270

Photo Credits

Cover, ©Robert Tringali, Jr./Sportschrome; 5, 6, AP/Wide World; 8, ©Robert Tringali, Jr./Sportschrome; 10, AP/Wide World; 11, Courtesy Don Shula family; 13, UPI Bettmann; 15, 17, AP/Wide World; 18, UPI/ Bettmann; 20 AP/Wide World; 22, Focus on Sports; 24, 26, AP/Wide World; 27, ©Mickey Palmer/Focus on Sports; 29, UPI/Bettmann; 30, Focus on Sports; 33, ©Brian Drake/Sportschrome; 34, AP/Wide World; 37, Sportschrome; 38, ©Mitchell B. Reibel/Sports Photo Masters, Inc.; 40 (both photos, 43, 47, AP/Wide World)

Project Editors: Shari Joffe and Mark Friedman
Design: Beth Herman Design Associates
Photo Editor: Jan Izzo

Library of Congress Cataloging-in-Publication Data

Stein, R Conrad.
    Don Shula: football's winningest coach / by R. Conrad Stein.
        p. cm. – (Sports stars)
    ISBN 0-516-04385-4
    1. Shula, Don, 1930- –Juvenile literature. 2. Football coaches– United States–Biography–Juvenile literature. [1. Shula, Don, 1930- . 2. Football coaches.] I. Title. II. Series.
GV939.S46S74   1994
796.332'092–dc20
[B]   94-9915
                                                                        CIP
                                                                        AC

Copyright 1994 by Childrens Press®, Inc.
All rights reserved. Published simultaneously in Canada.
Printed in the United States of America.
1 2 3 4 5 6 7 8 9 10 R 03 02 01 00 99 98 97 96 95 94

DON SHULA

FOOTBALL'S WINNINGEST COACH

It was an amazing scene. The home team trailed in the fourth quarter, but the crowd was cheering for the visiting team's coach: "Shu-LA! Shu-LA! Shu-LA!" And this was in Philadelphia, where people have booed their own cheerleaders.

This contest, played on November 14, 1993, was a game so dramatic that even the cranky Philadelphia fans could appreciate it. When the final gun sounded, the Miami Dolphins beat the Philadelphia Eagles 19-14. The triumph gave Miami coach Don Shula 325 career wins, one more than Chicago Bears' legend George Halas. Shula was now the winningest coach in pro football history.

Coach Shula watches over a Dolphins' practice; Shula is known for his intensity and devotion to hard work.

In the Miami locker room, the players celebrated. One would think they had just won the Super Bowl. Coach Shula then waved his arms at the team. "Now," he said, "we've got to go on."

It was a Shula message understood by everyone. There was another game next week. The team still had work to do. Working hard is a Shula trademark.

Don and his parents in 1973

Don Shula was born to a hardworking family on January 4, 1930. His father was an immigrant from Hungary. The Shulas lived in Painesville, Ohio, a town on the banks of Lake Erie. Don's father was a commercial fisherman. He wanted his son to follow in the same trade. But when Don went out on his father's fishing boat, he became miserably seasick. Shula remembered, "Dad said, 'You'll get over it.' Every time we went out he said that, 'You'll get over it.' Well, I never got over it."

★ ★ ★

So young Don Shula decided he was not destined to be a fisherman. His interests drifted to sports. He was a fine athlete and a natural leader on the playing field. In high school he starred in football, basketball, and baseball. He played sports with a special brand of fury. He hated to lose. As a younger child he used to cry when he lost card games with his grandmother. In high school, he could not bottle up and hide his passion to win. He often told other kids how to play their positions. "The coaches didn't always like it," Shula remembered, "but they put up with me."

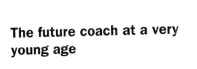

The future coach at a very young age

11

After high school, Shula enrolled at John Carroll College in Cleveland. It was a Catholic school, in keeping with his beliefs. Even today he attends Mass daily. He explains, "I enjoy going to Mass, thinking about Christ, giving thanks. I consider it part of my day."

Shula played halfback on John Carroll's football team. He had a good, but not an outstanding college football career. He lacked the blazing speed needed to be a breakaway running back. After graduating from college, he was chosen by the Cleveland Browns in the ninth round of the pro football draft.

At Cleveland, Shula met Paul Brown. Brown was one of the coaches who had founded pro football. He was as much a legend as George Halas. Shula later said, "Brown was the single greatest influence in my life. As a coach that man was able to bring the classroom to the football field."

Don Shula (white helmet) breaks up a pass in a 1951 NFL game.

Shula was a defensive back with Cleveland. He was a superb tackler, but more importantly, he emerged as the leader of the defensive backfield. Coach Brown assigned Shula to call defensive signals. That job was normally given to a linebacker.

Shula's lack of speed continued to haunt him in the pros. In 1953, he was traded to the Baltimore Colts (now the Indianapolis Colts), where he played for several years. Shula's playing career ended in 1957 with Washington. He then signed on as a college assistant coach at the University of Virginia. Shula also fell in love and married Dorothy Bartish, a grade-school teacher. In 1959, their first son, David, was born. David would later add football honors to the Shula family.

The Shula clan in 1973

In early 1963, a minor miracle transformed Don Shula's life.

Baltimore Colts owner Carroll Rosenbloom needed a dynamic new coach to revive his faltering team. Rosenbloom asked his leading player, Gino Marchetti, for a recommendation. Marchetti immediately thought of his ex-teammate. He told Rosenbloom, "There's only one man for the job, Don Shula."

The suggestion seemed absurd. At the time, Shula was working as an assistant with the Detroit Lions. He was only 33 years old. Dozens of coaches around the league had far more experience. Still, the Colts owner nodded and said, "Okay, I'll give him a try." And Don Shula became the youngest head coach in pro football history.

Coach Shula diagrams a play for the Colts' two top offensive stars, Johnny Unitas (left) and Lenny Moore.

In his first season, Shula brought a new spirit to Baltimore. He insisted his players pay attention to detail, avoid mental mistakes, and above all, work hard. He could be strict. He was never afraid to "chew out" a player, even in front of teammates. "He was strong, demanding, exact," Colts' halfback Tom Matte remembered. "He didn't mince any words. You had to have thick skin to play for him."

On the field, Shula emphasized basic football
— blocking and tackling, nothing fancy. Yet he
was able to bend the rules when circumstances
demanded. Late in the 1965 season, he lost
two quarterbacks. First his star, John Unitas,
was injured; then his backup, Gary Cuozzo,
was knocked out of the lineup for the season.
So Shula put little-used halfback Tom Matte
in as quarterback. Matte had never played
quarterback in his pro career. With Matte
as the "instant quarterback," the Colts won
a crucial game against the Los Angeles Rams
and then barely lost a playoff game to the Green
Bay Packers. The 1965 "instant quarterback"
championship contest is now considered to be
one of the most exciting games ever played in
pro football.

Don Shula led Baltimore to the playoffs three times. In 1965, the Colts were beaten by the Green Bay Packers, coached by the legendary Vince Lombardi (right).

★ ★ ★

Shula remained head coach of the Baltimore Colts for seven years. He never had a losing season. In 1969, he led the Colts to the Super Bowl. Because of his outstanding record, he was coveted by other teams. Miami offered him a lucrative contract. In 1970, Shula signed and took charge of the Dolphins.

The Dolphins were born as an expansion club in 1966. Their first four seasons resulted in a dismal record of 15 wins and 56 losses. Fewer than 30,000 fans bothered to attend their games. The franchise was losing millions of dollars. "I'm no miracle worker," Shula told the Miami media. "I don't have a magic formula . . . I'm just a guy who rolls up his sleeves and goes to work."

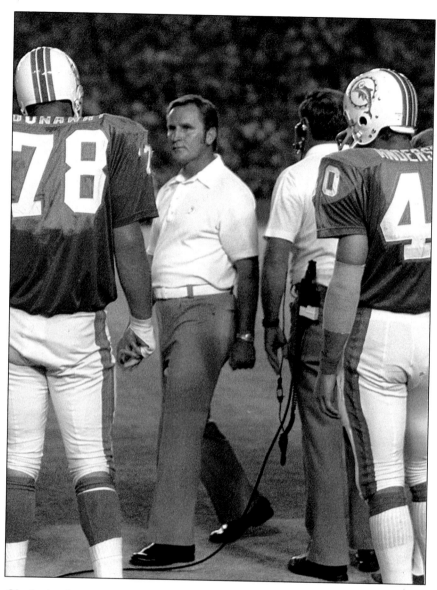

Shula took command of the Dolphins in 1970 and immediately whipped them into shape.

Once more, Shula proved that hard work can produce miracles. He analyzed the strengths and weaknesses of his players by studying hours of game film. When training camp began, he demanded that his men go through endless drills. His philosophy was simple: If we can't outplay the other guys, we'll outwork them. That simple philosophy reversed the fortunes of the Miami Dolphins. In 1969, the team had posted a record of 3 wins, 10 losses, and 1 tie. In Coach Shula's first year, they rang up an impressive 10-4 record.

And the best was yet to come.

Shula explodes with joy as Miami beats Kansas City in double overtime.

In 1971, Shula's second year, the Dolphins fought their way to the top of the AFC and went to the Super Bowl. The team's most incredible victory was a two-overtime dogfight in the AFC playoffs against Kansas City. The game lasted 82 minutes, 40 seconds — the longest game on record. It was finally won by Miami on a Garo Yepremian field goal.

While waiting for Super Bowl VI to begin, Shula received a surprising telephone call at 1:30 A.M. from President Richard Nixon. The president was a devoted football fan and called the coach to suggest he use a down-and-in pass play during the big game. Nixon's tip failed to help Shula's team. The Dolphins lost to the Dallas Cowboys 24-3.

The coach takes a victory ride on his players' shoulders after winning Super Bowl VII.

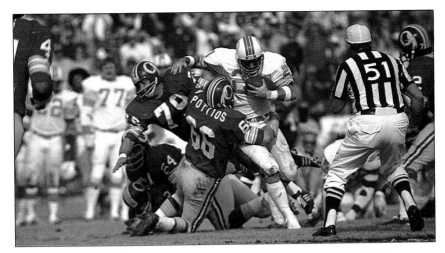

Miami's Jim Kiick scratches out some hard-fought yards in Super Bowl VII.

The 1972 Miami Dolphins were the most successful team ever to play in the NFL. Miami steamrolled over its opposition in the regular season, winning every game. In the playoffs, no team was able to stop Shula's warriors. Super Bowl VII was an easy victory as the Dolphins triumphed over Washington 14-7. Miami had posted a 17-0 record for the regular season and playoffs. Never before or since in modern NFL history has a team ripped through its opposition without suffering even one loss.

The next year, the Dolphins again dominated their opponents and reached the Super Bowl. It marked Shula's third straight Super Bowl appearance. In Super Bowl VIII, the Dolphins routed the Minnesota Vikings 24-7. They had now won two consecutive Super Bowls. All this from a team that finished in last place four years earlier — before Shula became head coach.

Football experts still marvel over the Dolphin powerhouse of the early 1970s. The team had very few star players. It won because it had the stamp of Don Shula all over it.

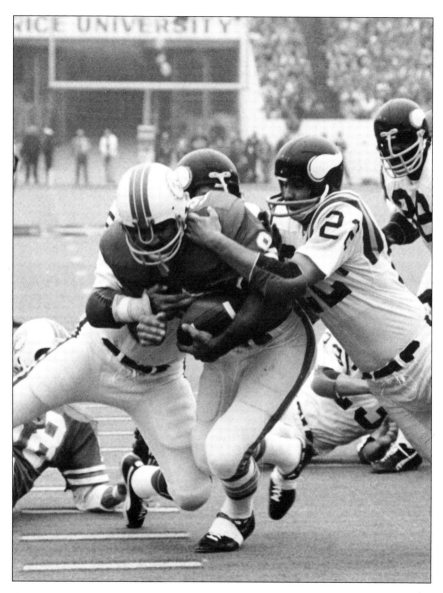

The Dolphins' Larry Csonka drags two Vikings into the end zone in Miami's Super Bowl VIII win.

"Butch Cassidy and the Sundance Kid" – Jim Kiick (#21) and
Larry Csonka (#39)

★ ★ ★

On offense, the Dolphins featured the
running of bulldozing fullback Larry Csonka
and halfback Jim Kiick. Neither man was
fast, but both were willing to scratch and
struggle for an extra yard, even with half
a dozen opposing players hanging on them.
Fans nicknamed Csonka and Kiick "Butch
Cassidy and the Sundance Kid," after a couple
of bad guys in a popular Western movie.

The defensive squad was so devoid of
standout players it was nicknamed the
"No Name Defense." But the unsung heroes
of defense played error-free football. Shula
detested mental blunders. Heaven help the
defensive lineman who foolishly jumped
offsides. He was ordered to the sidelines
where he had to face the icy stare of
Coach Shula.

Only one other team approached the amazing 17-0 record achieved by the 1971 Dolphins. That team was the 1985 Chicago Bears, led by fiery coach Mike Ditka. The Bears lost one game that year in their march toward a Super Bowl championship. Fittingly, the one loss came late in the season against Shula's Miami Dolphins. Later, Mike Ditka said of Shula, "He has won every which way a coach could win in this league. He had a run-oriented team in the early '70s, and now he has the best passing team with Dan Marino. . . . He has constantly bent his system to fit the talent of his players."

**Shula plots strategy with his son, David, who was a Dolphins'
assistant coach in the 1980s.**

--- ★ ★ ★ ---

Ditka pointed out a key reason why Shula has succeeded year after year. He evaluates his players, builds plays around their talents, and molds a winner. If he has an outstanding quarterback, he will emphasize a passing attack. If lineblocking is his team's strength, he will go to a running game. Shula enjoys playing poker in his spare time. Like any poker player, he knows he must play with the hand he is dealt.

Another cornerstone to Shula's success is his ability to evaluate talent. Shula needed a quarterback when the 1983 pro football draft began. By the time it was Miami's turn to pick, all the headliner quarterbacks were gone. No matter — Shula chose a relatively unsung guy from the University of Pittsburgh named Dan Marino.

★ ★ ★

When most scouts had seen Dan Marino play college ball at Pittsburgh, they did not anticipate that he would be an impact quarterback in the NFL. When Don Shula was asked why he had chosen Marino, Shula smiled and said, "He just had a twinkle in his eye that I liked."

In addition to seeing "a twinkle" in Marino's eye, Shula observed that he had a superb arm and unlimited talent that could be harnessed with good coaching. Some scouts and sportswriters disagreed. The word on Marino was that he was "pushing" the ball rather than firing it downfield. But Don Shula read the player differently. He said, "All I could see was how quickly he let [the ball] go, and how tremendous his peripheral vision seemed to be."

Coach Shula and his star quarterback, Dan Marino

Dan Marino reads the field in Super Bowl XIX.

★ ★ ★

As usual, Shula was right in his evaluation. Dan Marino entered the league and became an immediate star. He made the AFC All-Pro team in his rookie year. Shula added equally spectacular receivers for Marino to throw to: Mark Clayton and Mark Duper. With Marino, Clayton, and Duper leading the attack, the Dolphins developed an awesome offensive attack. In the mid-1980s, Marino could not be stopped, and Shula's Dolphins were again on top.

In 1984-85, Miami reached Super Bowl XIX. It was Don Shula's sixth Super Bowl as head coach, another record. His Dolphins faced the San Francisco 49ers — a spectacular matchup between Dan Marino and Joe Montana, the NFL's other top quarterback. But on this day, Montana was unstoppable, and the 49ers trounced Miami 38-16.

In the 1970s, teenager David Shula helped his dad on the sidelines during Dolphins games (top); in the 1990s, he became an NFL head coach (left).

In 1991, David Shula (Don's son) was named head coach of the Cincinnati Bengals. David had played briefly as a wide receiver for the Colts. He then coached as an assistant with the Dolphins and the Cowboys before taking over the top job with the Bengals. David and Don were the first father-and-son duo of head coaches in NFL history. In 1993, another Shula son, Mike, became an NFL assistant coach. Will the day come when three Shulas are at the helm of NFL teams?

Tragedy struck the Shula home in February 1991, when Dorothy, Don's wife of 33 years, died of cancer. It was the first time the five Shula children ever saw their father cry. His daughter Donna said, "It was terrible grief beyond words. He was lost without my mother."

———————————— ★ ★ ★ ————————————

Drawing on the support of his family and his strong faith in God, Don Shula eventually pulled out of his depression. He still dearly missed Dorothy, but he learned how to proceed with life without her. Happier times returned in 1993, when Shula remarried.

Those close to Don and his family claim the coach has mellowed over the years. One day, his six-year-old granddaughter, Lindsey, watched the news on television with her grandfather. The sports segment showed replays of a Dolphin loss. "Boy, Grandpa," said Lindsey, "the Dolphins sure stunk." In the past, such a statement from a six-year-old would have made Don furious — not at the child, but at his team. After all, if even a kid could detect a poor performance, the team must have really stunk.

But instead of getting mad, the coach listened to his granddaughter's criticism with a broad smile. Then he broke into a hearty laugh — as if to say, "What the heck, it's only a game."

Don Shula gets a much-deserved kiss from wife Mary Anne after the coach posted his record 325th victory.

★ ★ ★

Chronology

1930 – Don Shula is born on January 4 in Grand River, Ohio.

1948 – Shula becomes a starting halfback for John Carroll University. He plays with intensity, but lacks the speed to be a star.

1951 – Don is chosen by the Cleveland Browns in the ninth round of the pro football draft.

1953 – Shula is traded to Baltimore Colts.

1957 – Shula's playing career ends with the Washington Redskins.

1958 – Shula becomes assistant coach at University of Virginia.

1959 – Shula is an assistant coach at University of Kentucky.

1960 – Shula is an assistant coach with the NFL's Detroit Lions.

★ ★ ★

1963 – Shula is named head coach of the Baltimore Colts.
At 33, he is the youngest head coach in NFL history.
On September 22, he wins his first game when
Baltimore defeats San Francisco, 20-14.

1964 – Shula's Colts win the NFL's Western Conference, but lose
the championship game to Cleveland 27-0.

1968 – December 29: The Colts win the NFL championship,
beating Cleveland 34-0.

1969 – January 12: Baltimore loses to the New York Jets in
Super Bowl III.

1970 – Shula is named head coach of the last-place Miami
Dolphins.

1972-1973 – The Dolphins finish the regular season with
a 14-0 record. They remain unbeaten in the playoffs and
win Super Bowl VII over Washington on January 14, 1973.
Their 17-0 mark is the best record ever achieved by an
NFL team.

1974 – January 13: Miami beats Minnesota 24-7 in Super Bowl VIII.

1976 – September 26: Shula notches his 150th career coaching victory.

1983 – January 30: Shula's Dolphins lose 27-17 to Washington in Super Bowl XVII.

1985 – January 20: In Shula's sixth Super Bowl as head coach, Miami loses to San Francisco 38-16 in Super Bowl XIX.
  – November 24: Shula records his 250th career coaching victory.

1991 – Son David Shula is named head coach of the Cincinnati Bengals.

1993 – The Dolphins defeat Philadelphia 19-14, giving Don Shula his 325th career coaching victory, the most ever by an NFL head coach.

★ ★ ★

About the Author

R. Conrad Stein was born in Chicago. He attended the University of Illinois, where he received a degree in history. He is the author of many books for young readers.

Mr. Stein has been an avid pro football fan for years. He has followed Don Shula's career since Shula first took over the Baltimore Colts. Mr. Stein has always admired Don Shula as a successful coach, and as a gentleman.